GOD IS ENERGY. DO YOU BELIEVE? 3

...for it is by the grace of God that you have been saved...

SEMISI PULE

This book is based on the apostle Paul's letter
to the Ephesians, Chapter 2 verse 8.

Ephesians 2:8

'For it is by grace you have been saved,
through- faith and this is not from yourselves,
it is a gift of God'.

CONTENT

INTRODUCTION

I would like to emphasize, first, that my books are about what I say about my understanding of the bible, Christianity, religion and science. I do not want to go to bible college, for 3 years, and learn what other people say about the bible and religion then write a book. I want to write them according to my understanding and what I say.

I have been going to church since I was about 11 years old. I am now 54 years old. I have been reading the bible and other books ever since. I am sure you would not want me to repeat what my lecturers at college say, you want to read what I have to say. I understand what Ministers of Christian churches might say, but I feel that they should look at the world 'with different eyes'. The world is made up of 7 billion people and only about half of them are Christians. We all know God does grant his favors without prejudice. It rains, shines and crops produce the same harvests whether you are a Christian or not.

CHAPTER 1. GRACE

Saul who was also known as Paul was a persecutor of the early Christians. He was on his way to Damascus, in Syria, with permission from the High Priests in Jerusalem to arrest the Christians in Damascus and put them in chains. Acts 9: 1-19 tells the story of the conversion of Paul when he was struck down by Jesus. Paul was blinded and was taken by his co-travellers to a house in Damascus. He was instructed by Jesus, in a vision, to receive a man by the name of Ananias. A disciple who will restore his eyesight.

Jesus also instructed Ananias, in a vision, to go and see Paul and put his hands on his head and restore his sight in his name.

Ananias protested that Paul is a known prosecutor of Christians but Jesus told him in Acts 9:15-16.

'Go! This man is my chosen instrument to carry my name before the Gentiles and their kings and before the people of Israel. I must

show him how much he must suffer for my name'.

It was Paul, filled with the Holy Spirit, who immediately preached the Gospel and spread the name of Jesus, Acts 9: 19-31.

In all his epistles or letters to the Churches in Asia which includes part of present day Turkey (Colosse, Epheseus, Galatia) and Greece (Corinth, Phillipi, Thessalonica) he wished them the grace of God in every letter. At the beginning and end.

The other apostles Matthew, Mark, Luke, John, James, Peter, although they mention grace in their works, did not put a lot of emphasis on grace as Paul did. It was Paul who repeatedly greeted his audience with emphasis on grace as well as the end.

In Chapters 1-7, we shall explore the conversion of Paul and the meaning of Ephesians 2:8. He was a prolific writer. In fact, most of the books in the new Testament were written by him.

Why was God's grace mentioned so many times and emphasized by Paul?.

Grace is described by the Oxford Dictionary as 'free and unearned favor of God'. This status is very much sought after by believers because the favor of God will bring unlimited blessings on themselves. Blessings can include wealth, good health, love of others and many other things.

How does God pour his blessings or favor on the believers? We shall answer this question in this book.

The conversion of Saul does suggest that Jesus send Ananias to heal Saul in a vision. Saul was also instructed in a vision to receive Ananias, a disciple, who cured his blindness.

Saul was immediately converted and became a believer. He began preaching the gospel, to the disbelief of the High Priests who employed him to persecute the Christians.

Saul's adventures reveals a lot about his belief in the grace of God. Upon his conversion and preaching, the High Priests and their supporters immediately planned to kill him. It was only the quick action of his fellow Christians that saved his life....many times.

In his first letter to the Corinthians he began in verse 3, "Grace and peace to you from God our father and the Lord Jesus Christ".

Then it ends in Corinthians 16:23 'The grace of the Lord Jesus be with you'.

In 2 Corinthians 1:2 'Grace and peace to you from God our Father and the Lord Jesus Christ'. Ending in 13:14 'May the grace of the Lord Jesus Christ and the love of God, and the fellowship of the Holy Spirit be with you all.

The same or similar greetings, and endings, are used in his letters to the Galatians, Ephesians, Philippians, Colossians, Thessalonians, Timothy, Titus, Philemon even the ending of the book of Hebrews.

It must be that Paul felt that his life belong to Jesus and it is only by the Lord's grace or favor and permission that he is allowed to live and spread the gospel.

His boundless energy is obvious in his ministry and writings to his fellow Christians.

Ananias vision of Jesus and his message was probably Paul's driving force. Jesus said;

'This man is my chosen instrument to carry my name before the Gentiles and their kings and before the people of Israel. I must show him how much he must suffer for my name'.

Indeed Paul's suffering was great. Immediately, upon his conversion in Damascus, the Chief Priest's Jewish supporters planned to kill him. They watched the gates closely to catch him but his fellow Christians lowered him through an opening in the city wall and he escaped to Jerusalem.

The disciples in Jerusalem were all afraid of him, not really believing that he has become a Christian. Paul preached boldly in the name of Jesus and debated with the Grecian Jews who conspired to kill him. The disciples helped him escape to Tarsus where he is from. The bible say that peace came upon the Christians in Judea, Galilee and Samaria, all part of Palestine or present day Israel. The Holy Spirit strengthened and encouraged the Christians who grew in numbers.

The bible indicated that Paul was a Jew from Tarsus. The city is located in modern day Turkey, but was probably referred to as Galatia in the days of the bible. It does indicate the great distances that the disciples traveled. All the way up to modern day Greece. The letters to Christian churches in Corinth, Phillipi and Thessalonica suggest the disciples were there preaching and establishing those churches. They are cities in modern day Greece. Corinth and Thessalonica are still there to-day. Phillipi does not appear on the map of modern Greece.

The conversion of Paul was on the way to Damascus, the capital of modern Syria. Paul's healing by Ananias was in Damascus. Ananias was probably a Syrian Jew.

It appears there were pockets of Jews in all the destinations of Paul's letters who were preaching and converting locals to Christianity,

When Jesus taught his disciples how to pray he said;

'Our father which art in heaven
Hallowed be thy name
Thy Kingdom come
Thy will be done
On earth as it is in heaven
Give us this day our daily bread
And forgive us our trespasses
As we forgive them
That trespass against us
Lead us not into temptation
And deliver us from evil
For thine is the kingdom
The power and the glory
For ever and ever,
Amen.

Jesus made it obvious why Paul thinks that the grace of God is the most important blessing. The Lord's prayer, as taught by Jesus to his disciples, includes all the important blessings; 1. sustenance of the body and soul 2. forgiveness of sins 3. Avoidance of temptation and 4. deliverance from evil.

It does not include clothes, shelter or any other necessity. Perhaps you no not need them in 'the kingdom on earth'. There is a suggestion that the kingdom on earth is a spiritual rather than physical kingdom.

As the prayer requests;

'Thy Kingdom come
Thy will be done on earth'

Clearly, the Lord's prayer is a request for divine favors which Paul emphasize so much in his letters.

As he writes in Ephesians 2:8

'For it is by grace that you have been saved,
through faith-and this is not from yourselves,
it is a gift of God'.

What is *the Kingdom on earth* mentioned in the Lord's prayer?

Is it the second coming of Christ or the Holy Spirit?

When Jesus ascent to heaven and sent the
Holy Spirit, something miraculous happened.
The disciples were able to perform miracles in
the name of Christ. Paul was filled with the
Holy Spirit when he began preaching boldly
in Jerusalem and where ever he went even
debating with Grecian Jews who almost killed
him for his belief in Christ.

Paul understood God's favor or grace allowed
him to;

1. Escape his enemies 2. Write many of the
epistles 3. Spread the gospel

He believed that his life was *a favor from God.*

To-day there are 3,000,000,000 (3 billion) or
more Christians or followers of the teachings
of Jesus Christ. The whole world, all 7 billion
inhabitants of the earth are affected by the
teachings of Christ and his followers in some
way.

I believe that is what the Lord's prayer meant.... '*thy Kingdom come, thy will be done on earth as it is in heaven*'.

The Kingdom on Earth are the 3 billion followers of Jesus Christ, after 2,000 years from his ministry on earth. The Christians are now combined under the World Council of Christian Churches. It is a sure sign that the Christians, their churches, church organizations, church communities, homes and individuals make up the 'Kingdom on Earth'.

It is a fact that the Christian countries are the wealthiest and most advanced technologically in the world. It is the unearned favor or grace of the Lord Jesus Christ that allows them to '*reap the harvests of the earth*'. Christians are being guided by the Holy Spirit so they receive the full blessings or the favor of God.

Grace is also mentioned in James 4:6-7,

But he gives us more grace. That is why the scriptures says:

'God opposes the proud but gives grace to the humble'. Submit yourselves then to God. Resist the devil and he will flee.

In 1 Timothy 1:12-14, Paul made it clear why the grace of Jesus Christ was so important to him. He writes;

'I thank Jesus Christ our Lord, who has given me the strength, that he considered me faithful, appointing me to his service. Even though I was once a blasphemer and a persecutor and a violent man, I was shown mercy because I acted in ignorance and unbelief. The grace of our Lord was poured out on me abundantly, along with the faith and the love that are in Christ Jesus'.

At the beginning and end of most of his epistles he mentioned grace . In his letter to Titus 3:15, he writes;

'Everyone with me sends you greetings. Greet those who love us in the faith. Grace be with you all'.

In his letter to Philemon 1:25, he writes;

' The grace of the Lord Jesus Christ be with your spirit'.

Hebrew 13:25;

'Grace be with you all'

1 Thessalonians 5:28;

'The grace of our Lord Jesus Christ be with you'.

Galatians 2:21;

'I do not set aside the grace of God, for if righteousness could be gained through the law, Christ died for nothing'.

Paul believed that righteousness is gained through Christ not the law. It is by grace alone that makes the true believer.

1 Corinthians 15:9-11;

'For I am the least of the apostles and do not even deserve to be called an apostle, because

I persecuted the church of God. But by the grace of God I am what I am, and his grace to me was not without effect. No, I worked harder than all of them-yet not I, but the grace of God that was with me. Whether, then, it was I or they, this is what we preach, and this is what you believed.

Paul explains why he wrote so many epistles and why he worked harder than all the other apostles. He probably traveled to all the destinations of his epistles in modern Turkey and Greece, great distances to travel on foot. It is 'by the grace of God that was with him and effected his transformation and work'.

2 Corinthians13:14;

'May the grace of the Lord Jesus Christ, and the love of God, and the fellowship of the Holy Spirit be with you all'.

and Revelations 22:21;

'The grace of the Lord Jesus be with God's people.   Amen'.

Grace is very important in the spiritual wellness of the Christian.

The favor of God also includes love in 1 Corinthian 13:1-13;

This is one of Paul's most famous passages in his epistles. In verse 4-7 he writes;

'Love is patient, love is kind. It does not envy, it does not boast, it is not proud. It is not rude, it is not self-seeking, it is not easily angered, it keeps no record of wrongs. Love does not delight in evil but rejoices with truth. It always protects, always trusts, always hopes, always perseveres.

and Roman 5:8;

'But God demonstrates his love for us in this: While we were still sinners, Christ died for us'.

God's grace include wisdom. In James 1:5 he writes;

'If any of you lacks wisdom, he should ask

God who gives generously to all without finding fault, and it will be given to him'.

God's grace include perseverance. In James 1:3-4,12 he writes;

Verse 3-4 - *'Because you know that the testing of your faith develops perseverance. Perseverance must finish its work so that you may be mature and complete, not lacking anything'.*

Verse 12 - *'Blessed is the man who perseveres under trial, because when he has stood the test, he will receive the crown of life that God has promised to those who love him'.*

In James 5:11;

'As you know, we consider blessed those who have persevered. You have heard of Job's perseverance and have seen what the Lord finally brought about. The Lord is full of compassion and mercy'.

God's grace include patience. In James 5:7-8 he writes;

Verse 7-8 - *'Be patient, then, my brothers, until the Lords coming. See how the farmer waits for the land to yield its valuable crop and how patient he is for the autumn and spring rains. You too, be patient and stand firm, because the Lord's coming is near'* .

God's grace include freedom. In John 8:31-32 he writes;

'Jesus said, If you hold to my teaching, you are really my disciples. Then you will know the truth, and the truth will set you free'.

God's grace include abundant life. In John 10:10 Jesus said;

'The thief comes only to steal and kill and destroy; I have come so that they may have life and have it more abundantly'.

God's grace include rejoicing in the Lord's work. In Matthew 5:11-12 Jesus said;

'Blessed are you when people insult you, persecute you and falsely says all kinds of evil against you because of me. Rejoice and be glad, because great is your reward in heaven, for in the same way they persecuted the prophets who were before you'.

God's grace include salvation by the teachings of Christ. In James 1:19-21, he writes;

'Everyone should be quick to listen, slow to speak and slow to become angry, for man's anger does not bring about the righteous life that God desires. Therefore, get rid of all moral filth and the evil that is so prevalent and humbly accept the word planted in you, which can save you'.

John 3:16 also emphasizes that belief or faith in Christ and his teachings is man's only hope of salvation. This is a point made by Paul in Romans 5:8 and Ephesians 2:8.

John writes;

'For God so loved the world, he gave his one and only son, that whoever believes in him shall not perish but have eternal life'.

Salvation as emphasized by James and John is belief and faith and action of the teachings of Jesus Christ, one of the blessings or favor of God. The grace that Paul valued so much.

The life giving rain and sunshine, fertile soil, fruitful trees, milk and honey are all part of the favor and grace of God, for they are his creations.

No wonder Paul wished grace on all his Christian brothers. As the hymn suggest;

'Amazing grace how sweet the sound,
That saved a wretch like me,
I once was lost but now I am found,
Was blind but now I see'.

Paul's salvation and conversion is purely by the grace of Jesus Christ.

CHAPTER 2. SAVED!

Being saved in the Christian sense is protecting a person's soul from eternal damnation. The salvation of the Christian is granted through faith in the death and resurrection of Christ as revealed in John 3:16.

Proof of the death and resurrection of Christ are mentioned, not only in the 4 gospels of Matthew, Mark, Luke and John but also in Paul's letters. In 1 Corinthians 15:3-8, he writes;

'For what I received I pass on to you as of first importance; that Christ died for our sins according to the Scriptures, that he was buried, that he was raised on the third day according to the Scriptures, and that he appeared to Peter, and then to the Twelve. After that, he appeared to more than 500 of the brothers at the same time, most of whom are still living, though some have fallen asleep. Then he appeared to James, then to all the apostles, and last of all he appeared to me also'.

Salvation from eternal damnation is the goal of the Christian faith. It is the whole objective of becoming a Christian, to be saved through faith in Jesus Christ.

Paul does say in his epistle that though *'all have died with Adam, they have now arisen with Jesus'*. The original sin and disobedience of Adam is the cause of man' s eternal exclusion from paradise or the Garden of Eden. The gospel of Jesus is much more than that. Much, much more than *'returning man to the Garden of Eden'*.

Jesus Christ began and promoted education and philosophy. This mission was continued by the Christian missionaries to all parts of the world. In the small Pacific Island country of Tonga, it was the missionaries that introduced education, modern government, music, mathematics and ethical ways of living. Education became the most revered and desired goal in the Tongan parents wish list for their children.

It is very obvious from the writings of the

apostles that the Holy Spirit guides them in what they say. This is very, very clear with Paul's letters. They are very concise and with deep explanations of what it is to be a Christian and in the service of Jesus Christ. The bible does indicate that Paul was *'filled with the Holy Spirit that guide him in everything he does'*.

Paul's writings about love, money, grace and many other important topics are the cornerstones of Christianity to-day. Ananias's vision became real. Jesus did use Paul as his *'instrument to spread his gospel to the Gentiles and their kings....*and he was also taught how much he must suffer in the name of Christ'.

Consider Paul's letter in 1 Timothy 6:10;

'For the love of money is a root of all kinds of evil'.

This is just one of his many famous quotes, which has generated discussions and debates around the world.

I was in a debate in 4th form in Tonga High School about that very quote from Paul's epistle. Is money the root of all evils?. At the time I did not know it was a quote from the letter by Paul to Timothy, whom he called his *'son in the faith'*.

Paul was, again, very specific about grace. He began by writing;

'To Timothy my true son in the faith:

Grace, mercy and peace from God the father and Christ Jesus our Lord'.

Of the 27 books in the New Testament, Paul wrote, at least, 14 of them. His epistles are distinct because of his emphasis on wishing grace and blessings at the beginning and end of his letters. None of the other apostles had put so much emphasis on grace as he did. It is also clear from his work that he was more active than the others as an evangelist of Christ.

In that sense, the ending of the book of Revelations;

'The grace of the Lord Jesus be with God's people.   Amen'

....is a typical ending used often by the apostle Paul. Perhaps he had a hand in writing the book of Revelations?.

Since he was the most prolific of all the New Testament writers, it may be that Paul was a scholar. His association with the High Priests during his 'rebellious' days and his debates with the Grecian Jews suggest that he was a learned man.....his violent opposition to the teachings of Christ may have been precipitated by his learning in the traditional Jewish religion.

Jewish religion is very different from Christianity. It is the cause of the crucifixion of Jesus Christ because he was teaching the Jews something totally different and it was the Jewish High Priests who asked the Romans to crucify him. They were scared of his teachings that it might take away their authority as the 'teachers and caretakers of Jewish religion and knowledge'.

The Romans were reluctant to kill Jesus because their laws were more civilized than the Jews. They insisted that he must be tried in a Roman court of law....they did not find him guilty of anything.....and even decided to 'wash their hands' from his case. They even asked the Jewish crowds who they should crucify....Jesus or another common criminal....and the Jewish crowds chose Jesus to be crucified.....presumably at the influence of the Jewish High Priests.

On the cross on Calvary, one of the criminals crucified with him asked him... "if you are the Son of God why don't you save yourself and us?".

The other criminal rebuked him and said. "We are common criminals. This man is innocent". Then he said to Jesus. "Lord when your kingdom comes please remember me, I am a sinner".

And Jesus replied, "To-day you will be in paradise with me".

This is the basis of the Christian salvation. It is not saving the body from death but the spirit from eternal damnation. When Jesus said they will be in paradise....he meant their souls or spirits will be in paradise. The body will rot and return to the earth but their spirits will live forever in paradise or heaven.

Paul did mention it in his letters that *'the heavenly body has its own splendor'*. It is referred to as the Higher Being in book 2 of this series. Paul was a man who saw Jesus and he probably saw Jesus in his 'heavenly body'...which is why he wrote that the heavenly body has its own 'splendor' which is different from the splendor of the earth body.

There is something really important in faith as the most important step towards being saved as a Christian. You have to believe in Jesus Christ. That he died on the cross for your sins and rose again in three days. He conquered death so that man can live forever. Man will no longer die for all eternity. Although his earth body will rot and return to the earth, his heavenly body will live forever.
This is what salvation or being saved in the

Christian sense mean. The Hindus call it 'returning to the Cosmic Spirit'.

In Hindu religion, the whole objective of life is to 'escape the cycle of death and rebirth that we are caught in on earth and escape to the Cosmic Spirit'. It is exactly the same principle as being saved in the Christian sense.

Hindus believe that the earth body is a punishment for one's bad karma in previous lives. That only good deeds will allow the soul to escape the continuous death and rebirth and return to the Cosmic Spirit or God.

It is very similar to 'death through Adam's original sin and rising again, from the dead, with Christ'

I have discussed this in book 2...that the four major religions of the world Christianity, Islam, Hinduism and Buddhism all have similar beliefs in the salvation of man.

The destiny of man according to those 4 religions is to save the 'Eternal or Higher Being'.....the earthly body is disposable.

There are almost 7 billion people in those 4 religions combined....and they believe in eternal life and the salvation of the 'Higher Being'. Can they be wrong?.

In 1 Corinthians 15: 20-22 and 40, Paul describes why death and resurrection came about....and the differences in the earth body and heavenly body.

Verse 20-22.... *'But Christ has indeed been raised from the dead, the first fruits of those who have fallen asleep. For since death came through a man, the resurrection of the dead comes also through a man. For as in Adam all die, so in Christ all will be made alive'.*

Verse 40..... *'There are also heavenly bodies and there are earthly bodies; but the splendor of the heavenly bodies is one kind, and the splendor of the earthly bodies another'.*

CHAPTER 3. DAMNATION

'Damnation is the condemnation of the soul or spirit to eternal punishment in hell'.

Man died when Adam disobeyed God and was punished from paradise or the Garden of Eden. Christ came to give abundant life back to man and to save him from death by returning him to paradise.

As the apostle Paul wrote.... *as all have died with Adam now all rise from the dead with Jesus'*. It is possible that Adam and Eve were living in paradise, Garden of Eden or Heaven. Everything was provided for them. Then the serpent told them to eat the 'forbidden fruit' because they will become like God and know good and evil.

Adam and Eve were banished from Eden or paradise. The bible say that an angel with a flaming sword was put at the gate to the Garden of Eden so Adam and Eve cannot return there and eat from the 'fruit of eternal life'. It will make them like God and live forever.

Christ came to help man return to paradise, by showing him that it is possible for him to rise from the dead. By showing him that if he believes that Jesus died for Adam's sins and forgave him....he can return to paradise. He no longer need to eat from the 'fruit of eternal life', all he has to do, is 'believe'.

In John 11:25-26 Jesus said;

'I am the resurrection and the life. He who believes in me will live, even though he dies. And whoever lives and believes in me will never die'.

Jesus had said this to Martha, brother of Lazarus, after she had told him that Lazarus had died 4 days before.

Jesus had spent a lot of time with Mary and Martha and their brother Lazarus at Bethany, 2 miles from Jerusalem. The bible say he wept when he learned of the death of Lazarus, before he raised him from the dead. All the people who witnessed it were amazed and some reported the miracle to the Pharisees and High Priests....who immediately planned to kill him. They reasoned that if the people believed in Jesus, the Romans will remove their authority and perhaps the nation of Israel will be lost.

It is obvious from early Christian days that their worst enemy was the High Priest of Jewish religion. He wanted to protect his power as High Priest. If the people believe Jesus and his disciples, then his office of High Priest will be redundant. It seem that the excuse of..... 'fearing for the loss of the nation of Israel' was used to isolate and kill Jesus and the apostles.

The Romans were already ruling over the nation of Israel so it was already lost! Israel was already part of the Roman Empire. But the High Priest managed to convince the local Jews that if his office loses in an 'imagined battle' against Jesus and his disciples, the nation of Israel will be lost to the Rpmans.

Presumably, the High Priest was the 'law' and it was he who determines how Jewish people shall live their lives. His office was under threat from Jesus and his supporters because they are preaching something different to what he, the High Priest, is saying. So they must be killed.

The same kind of logic is still being used today in many countries where there are conflicts between religions. In the Middle East, the majority Islam religion is being used against the Christians there. Many Christians are executed because they are 'different' from the majority....just as the High Priest of Jewish religion wanted to execute Jesus and his disciples.

The present conflict in Israel between the Jews and Islam, in the form of Palestinians, can be traced to the same kind of logic. The majority Jews do not want any Moslems living there because they are saying something different to what they believe.

This is exactly the kind of 'eternal damnation' that Jesus and his disciples were preaching against. The kind of bad karma that man creates which will result in his endless rebirth to pain and suffering on earth, until his good deeds will exonerate him and he escapes back to God or the Cosmic Spirit.

After 5,000 years or more of religious teachings man has still not understood the main principle of it.

Eternal damnation include hatred. Jesus preached against it. In Matthew 5:43-44 Jesus said;

'You have heard that it was said, 'Love your neighbor and hate your enemy. But I tell you: love your enemies and pray for those that persecute you'.

Jesus knew the result of hatred is eternal damnation. The Hindus describe it better as 'bad karma' which will result in 'eternal damnation or being trapped in the endless cycle of birth and death on earth'. The spirit can only escape to the Cosmic Spirit or God if you do what Jesus recommends... *'love your enemies and pray for them'.* The 'good deeds' recommended in Hindu religion.

Eternal damnation is also a result of sin. It is described in John 8:34-35;

Jesus replied, 'I tell you the truth, everyone who sins is a slave to sin. Now a slave has no permanent place in the family, but a son belongs to it forever'.

In James 4:17 he writes;

'Anyone, then, who knows the good he ought to do and doesn't do it, sins.

Sin is like bad karma, it prevents one from reaching the ultimate goal of this existence; which is eternal life. Eternal life is only possible when you become one with God or the Cosmic Spirit. It is the eternity of God that becomes part of you and make you live forever.

When you sin, you are a slave to it. Sin as described in the bible as 'bad deeds' and the only recommendation as proposed by Hindus is 'good deeds' to escape from the slavery of sin.

Sin or bad deeds appear to be the only reason why many people do not reach their potential on earth and 'return to the Cosmic Spirit' thus living forever as part of God. Most people on earth know that sin is bad but it is difficult to live an exemplary life of pure 'sin free' existence.

This is why Jesus also emphasized that 'forgiveness' of man's sins is an important step to 'returning to the Cosmic Spirit'. Jesus died in order for man to be 'washed clean in his blood'....for man's sins to be forgiven so he can return to God. It makes it possible for man to have eternal life....or return to the Cosmic Spirit because his bad karma or sins has been wiped clean in the blood of Jesus Christ.

In New Zealand, the Government recently passed a law where some criminals will have their criminal record 'wiped clean' by the State. They are given a 'second chance' to rebuild their lives saving them from a lifetime of hardship caused by their criminal convictions. The media reported 500,000 New Zealanders benefited from that law change.

I consider that law change the most important legal development since they started making laws. The reason is simple. Good people who were 'wronged' by the State can live a good prosperous life again which were denied them when they had criminal convictions.

The criminal conviction prevent them from getting jobs, traveling to certain places, becoming involved in community work or even starting a business. Their criminal convictions will always be a barrier to anything they try to do for themselves.

What the 'clean slate' legislation does point out is that the State was wrong to convict those people in the first place. True it was the law....but then who makes the law?. 500,000 people were freed from that bondage by a simple change in legislation. Imagine what will happen if the State forgive everyone's trespasses or crimes against it? Probably, more than 1,000,000 people will benefit.

Those people suffered a lot of hardship at the hands of the State, but they were not compensated. Why? Because the State is a dead being, it does not have the capacity for love and compassion. The State does not care about those 500,000 people. All it did was pat itself on the back for that 'good deed'. But it was not a good deed....it was simply covering up its original mistakes.

Only God has the capacity for love and compassion. After he banished man from the Garden of Eden or paradise...because of the disobedience of Adam and Eve, he send his son Jesus Christ to compensate man for his sufferings and allow him to return to paradise. To return to the Cosmic Spirit. To escape the endless cycle of death and birth and suffering on earth.

Imagine what happens when God gives you a clean slate? When God forgives all the trespasses of all the 7 billion people on earth? It was only possible to give all the people of earth a clean slate when it was washed with the blood of Jesus Christ. The forgiveness of sin, the resurrection and everlasting life was only possible when the son, the sacrificial lamb volunteered. The son conquered death

and released everyone from bondage. Then he
send the Holy Spirit to guide man and help
him in his guest for eternal life.

Man no longer has to depend on his good
deeds to save him. Only his faith in Jesus
Christ, the resurrection, the forgiveness of sin
and eternal life is required.

CHAPTER 4. FAITH

'Faith is complete trust and confidence in the power of God'.

The power of faith is demonstrated in the story of the centurion in Matthew 8:5-17. Jesus came to Capernaum and a centurion came to him and asked him to help his servant who was paralyzed in bed with terrible suffering. Jesus wanted to go there but the centurion asked him to just *'say the word and he will be healed'*.

Jesus said to the centurion;

'Go! It will be done as you said it would'.
And his servant was healed at that very hour.

In Mark 11:22-24, the story of the fruitless fig unfolds. Jesus cursed it and it died. Peter was amazed, but Jesus told him that if he has faith in God and he believes with all his heart that it will happen, it will be done for him. If he ask God anything and believe it, it will happen for him.

He said;

Therefore, I tell you whatever you ask for in prayer, believe that you have received it and it will be yours.

In Galatians 2:20 Paul writes;

'I have been crucified with Christ and I no longer live, but Christ lives in me. The life I live in the body, I live by faith in the son of God, who loved me and gave himself for me.

This is probably the most important passage on faith in the bible and I will include all of it in this chapter because it is important for understanding what faith is about.

In Hebrew 11: 1-11 and 17, 20-25,27-30, faith in almost everything is listed. It begins;

Verses 1-11 - *'Now faith is being sure of what we hope for and certain of what we do not see. This is what the ancients were commended for.*

By faith we understand that the universe was formed at God's command, so what is seen was not made out of what was visible.

By faith Abel offered God a better sacrifice than Cain did. By faith he was commended as a righteous man when God spoke well of his offerings. And by faith he still speaks, even though he is dead.

By faith Enoch was taken from this life, so that he did not experience death; he could not be found, because God has taken him away. For before he was taken, he was commended as one who pleased God.

And without faith it is impossible to please God, because anyone who comes to him must believe that he exists and that he rewards those that earnestly seek him.

By faith Noah, when warned about things not yet not seen, in holy fear built an ark to save his family. By his faith he condemned the world and became heir of the righteousness that comes by faith.

By faith Abraham, when called to go to a place he would later receive as his inheritance, obeyed and went, even though he did not know where he was going. By faith he made his home in the promised land like a stranger in a foreign country; he lived in tents, as did Isaac and Jacob, who were heirs with him of the same promise. And so from this one man, and he was as good as dead, came descendants as numerous as the stars in the sky and as countless as the sand of the seashore.

Verses 17 - *By faith Abraham, when God tested him, offered Isaac as a sacrifice. He who had received the promises was about to sacrifice his one and only son.*

Verse 20 -25 *By faith Isaac blessed Jacob and Esau in regard to their future.*
By faith Jacob, when he was dying, blessed each of Joseph's sons,and worshiped as he leaned on the top of his staff.
By faith Joseph, when his end was near, spoke about the exodus of the Israelites from Egypt and gave instructions about his bones.
By faith Moses' parents hid him for 3 months after he was born, because they saw that he was no ordinary child and they were not

afraid of the king's edict.

By faith, Moses when he had grown up, refused to be known as the son of Pharaoh's daughter.He chose to be mistreated along with the people of God rather than to enjoy the pleasures of sin for a short time.

Verse 27 -30 -   *By faith he left Egypt not fearing the king's anger; he persevered because he saw him who is invisible.*
By faith he kept the Passover and the sprinkling of blood, so that the destroyer of the firstborn will not touch the firstborn of Israel.
By faith the people passed through the Red Sea as on dry land; but when the Egyptians tried to do so, they were drowned.

By faith, the walls of Jericho fell, after the people had marched around them for seven days.

Many other people like Gideon, Samson, David, Samuel and other prophets acts of faith are also mentioned in the bible.

Gideon was a Judge who was chosen by God to deliver Israel from its enemies and idol worship. He was famous for how he selected his soldiers to fight for Israel. His faith led him to victory.

Samson's faith allowed him to destroy his enemies by shaking and destroying the building with his own hands.

David's faith in the Lord allowed him to kill Goliath with a sling and pebble and led the Israel Army to win. His success made King Saul jealous who tried to kill David. David's faith in God brought destruction on the house of Saul and the prophet Samuel anointed him the new King of Israel.

Samuel's faith in God and David made him the most successful and famous of the King's of Israel. Even though he made mistakes God's favor never left him.

Faith plays a very important role in religion. It is the sole driving force in all religious activities. If the members lack faith, they will not be supporting the religion at all.

As demonstrated by these bible verses faith in God can move mountains.

Faith according to Jesus.

In John 14:15-24, Jesus promised his disciples the Holy Spirit, he will send to guide and help them. For it is only by faith they obey his commands. Those who do not love him will not have faith in him nor obey his commands.

"If you love me, you will obey what I command. And I will ask the Father, and he will give you another Counselor to be with you forever. The Spirit of Truth. The world cannot accept him, because it neither sees him nor knows him. But you know him, for he lives with you and will be in you. I will not leave you as orphans: I will come to you. Before long, the world will not see me any more, but will see me. Because I live, you also will live. On that day you will realize that I am in my Father, and you are in me, and I am in you. Whoever has my commands and obeys them, he is the one who loves me. He who loves me will be loved by my father, and I too

will love him and show myself to him.

Then Judas (not Judas Iscariot) said, "But Lord, why do you intend to show yourself to us and not to the world?"

Jesus replied, "If anyone loves me, he will obey my teaching. My Father will love him and make our home with him. He who does not love me will not obey my teaching. These words you hear are not my own; they belong to the Father who sent me".

Faith has a large element of love in it. As John wrote, Jesus was very specific about it.

"He who does not love me will not obey my teachings".

The Christian countries whose laws and constitutions are based on the teachings of Jesus Christ are very wealthy materially. It is true that this is the precipitation of the Christian faith. The major result of which is peace and prosperity.

Some Moslem countries who follow the

teachings of Muhammad are at war most of the time. And it is true also that the teachings of Muhammad precipitates this end result for its followers and believers. They say that Moslems believes...that non-believers in Islam....are infidels. They have to be eliminated. Some of the history points out that Islam spread more by conquest rather than conversion by faith.....and this is probably why there is so much conflict.

Although Islam, as I have mentioned in book 2 does resemble the Christian faith in summary, there is still a lot of differences in the detail.

Jesus did promise that God will 'make his home' with those who have faith in him;

"If anyone loves me, he will obey my teaching. My Father will love him and make our home with him. He who does not love me will not obey my teaching. These words you hear are not my own; they belong to the Father who sent me".

When God decides to make his home with

you, there is nothing in the world that is impossible. Good fortune and goodwill will fill your house forever.

This is emphasized in Psalm 23, the most famous of the 150 Psalms in the bible.

The Lord is my shepherd, I shall not be in want.
He makes me lie down in green pastures, he leads me beside quiet waters, he restores my soul.
He guides me in paths of righteousness for his name's sake.
Even though I walk through the valley of the shadow of death, I will fear no evil, for you are with me: your rod and staff they comfort me.
You prepare a table before me in the presence of my enemies.
You anoint my head with oil; my cup overflows.
Surely goodness and love will follow me all the days of my life, and <u>I will dwell in the house of the Lord forever.</u>

Many of the stories of the prophets and

people who have faith as explained in Hebrew
11 testify to the fact, that the Lord does
provide for those who believe or have faith in
him.
Faith and obedience also go hand in hand.
When Jesus promised the Holy Spirit he only
intended it as the reward of those who believe.
This is emphasized by Peter in Acts 5: 27-32.

*Having brought the apostles, they made them
appear before the Sanhedrin to be questioned
by the high priest. "We gave you strict orders
not to teach in his name," he said. "Yet you
have filled Jerusalem with your teaching and
are determined to make us guilty of this man's
blood."*

*Peter and the other apostles replied: "We
must obey God rather than men! The God of
our fathers raised Jesus from the dead -
whom you have killed by hanging him from a
tree. God exalted him to his own right hand
as Prince and Savior that he might give
repentance and forgiveness of sin to Israel.
We are witnesses of these things, and so is the
Holy Spirit, whom God has given to those
who obey him".*

The apostles were persecuted and killed by the Jewish high priest and his supporters, but as we witness to-day the Christian followers are about 3 billion in number to less than 10 million who follow the Jewish religion.

So it is the teachings of Christ that is the clear winner in this conflict. In fact, the only existence of the Jewish State to-day was through the goodwill and generosity of the Christians. If the Christians did not have the love and care taught by Christ they would not have stopped Hitler who was bent on exterminating the Jews. He had wiped out 6 million Jews in Europe and if he had won the war....he probably would have wiped out the Jews in the Middle East as well.

The Christians are also supporting and protecting Israel against the majority Moslems in the Middle East, as well.

We learn that the teachings of Christ does give life, freedom, prosperity and hope to the nations of the world. This example where Christians, who were once persecuted by the

Jews, have used Christ's love and teachings to save them from certain oblivion.

Faith is also an important element in knowing the way. In John 14:5-6; John writes;

Thomas said to him, "Lord we don't know where you are going, so how can we know the way?".

Jesus answered. "I am the way and the truth and the life. No one comes to the Father except through me".

The way is clear. Jesus is the way. Faith in him will show those who believe what to do. His promise to send the Holy Spirit to guide those who have faith in him does appear to be the key factor in 'finding the way'.

Christians are the peace keepers of the world to-day. They work hard and store food to feed the hungry of the world. Their wealth is not only intended for themselves but also to feed those who are hungry regardless of their religion and background. Christians believe in the guidance of the Holy Spirit and it shines like a beacon for the rest of the world to follow, without forcing other religions to join Christianity. Christians show them the love of Christ and that is enough.

The apostle James emphasizes 'faith and deeds' to show the world the love and teachings of Christ. In James 2: 14-18, James writes;

What good is it, my brothers, if a man claims to have faith but has no deeds? Can such faith save him? Suppose a brother or sister is without clothes and daily food. If one of you says to him, "Go, I wish you well keep warm and well fed," but does nothing about his physical needs, what good is it? In the same way, faith by itself, if it is not accompanied by action, is dead.
But someone will say, "You have faith I have deeds. Show me your faith without deeds, and I will show you my faith by what I do".

This is obviously a very important point in Christian charities. They must have faith and accompanied with action, for faith without action, in the apostle's words, is dead.

The apostle James also wrote about faith in healing. If one is sick he must pray and he will be healed.

In James 5: 13-16, he writes;

Is anyone of you in trouble? He should pray. Is anyone happy? Let him sing songs of praise. Is anyone of you sick? He should call the elders of the church to pray over him and anoint him with oil in the name of the Lord. And the prayer offered in faith will make the sick person well; the Lord will raise him up. If he has sinned, he will be forgiven. Therefore confess your sins to each other and pray for each other so that you may be healed. The prayer of a righteous man is powerful and effective".

Prayers of the faithful are well known around the world. The believers pray and ask God and what they ask is delivered to them. Jesus did say, "Ask and you will be given."

CHAPTER 5. GIFT OF GOD

...a present, willingly given to man without payment...Oxford Dictionary

The unconditional love and favor of the supreme being, the cosmic spirit, the creator of the universe is described by many books as the gift of God.

But there is more to it.

As written in John 3:16, man is also offered eternal life as a 'Gift of God'. Man through sin, was damned to die forever, but Christ came and died to conquer death so that man can live.

As the apostle Paul wrote...as all have died with Adam so shall rise again with Christ.

It seems that Adam and eve through their disobedience were banished to become mortals. Earning their bread through the sweat of their brow. Eve was punished to bear children in pain. Both were driven from the 'Garden of Eden' to live as nomads on earth and its meager offerings.

The bible does mention that Adam and Even were prevented from entering the 'Garden of Eden' again or they will eat from the tree of life and live forever.

In Genesis 4:21-24, it is written;

The Lord God made garments of skin for Adam and his wife and clothed them. And the Lord God said, "The man has now become like one of us, knowing good and evil. He must not be allowed to reach out his hand and take also from the tree of life and eat, and live forever."
So the Lord God banished him from the Garden of Eden to work the ground from which had been taken. After he drove the man out, he placed on the east side of the Garden of Eden a cherubim and a flaming sword flashing back and forth to guard the way to the tree.

Adam and Eve cannot return to the Garden of Eden. They cannot eat from the tree of eternal life as God has banished them. It is also written that Jesus came to give man life so that he may live abundantly....in addition....if he believes in him, he will also be rewarded with everlasting or eternal life.

That is a 'Gift of God'.

Adam, the first man's disobedience, has finally been forgiven through the son, and he may claim eternal life....not through the fruits of the tree of life in the Garden of Eden.....but through faith in Jesus Christ, the resurrection, the forgiveness of sin and eternity.

It is unclear what the bible mean by damnation and it has been explained in Chapter 3. So it is likely that the first man's disobedience is the reason and punishment to live a life as a mortal. After the son had secured man's forgiveness and conquered death, it was possible for man to return to the Garden of Eden, to claim his life as a God or an immortal being, referred to as 'The Higher Being' in book 2.

The Hindus refer to this as 'returning to the Cosmic Spirit or God of the Universe. In other words becoming one with God and living as an immortal being.

It is the destiny of man, as explained in book 2, to escape the cycle of sin, suffering and pain on earth and return to God.

In Jesus, salvation was possible simply through faith.

These are the elements of God's gift to man through the scriptures.

1. Hope - Hope is important to the poor, oppressed, distressed, suffering and others throughout the world. In 1 Peter 13 he writes;

Therefore prepare your minds for action: be self-controlled; set your hope fully on the grace to be given to you when Jesus Christ is revealed.

The grace of God is a gift. It is the eternal blessing and favor received through faith in Jesus Christ. We have seen this grace work wonders through the Christians throughout the world.

Jesus had commanded his disciples....*go and make every man on earth my disciples.*

And it has been implemented by St Peter and the apostles. There are now more than 3 billion people who are influenced by the grace of God. More than that....there are 7 billion people on earth who have found their lives have improved by the grace of God through the Christian action networks all over the world.

The advice of St James that their faith must be accompanied by their deeds have born fruits to-day. Christians do apply their faith through various charities and faith seminaries in almost every country. Distributing and implementing Gods grace wherever the poor, oppressed and suffering need help irrespective of their religion, culture, race, color and faith.

Sometimes we take God's grace for granted. God's favor on Christians is obvious for all to see. But as I mentioned many times in book 2 and in this book that the 'Gift of God', just like the life giving rain and the sunshine is available for all mankind. All they have to do is reach out to God and take it. That is the hope that Jesus Christ offers.

2. Holy - Being good or extra good is a desirable attribute in being a Christian. However, it is impossible for man to be holy unless he is 'washed in the blood of the lamb.' Every time he sins he is forgiven and made pure again.

In 1 Peter 1:14-16 he writes;

As obedient children, do not conform to the evil desires you had when you lived in ignorance. But just as he who called you is holy, so be holy in all you do; for it is written: "Be holy, because I am holy."

3. Joy - Joy in the Christian sense has a lot to do with salvation. He who has been saved from eternal damnation and the clutches of the devil feels joy because he is one with God. The apostle Luke writes about it.

In Luke 10: 18-20 Jesus said;

I saw Satan fall like lighting from heaven. I

have given you authority to trample on snakes and scorpions and to overcome all the power of the enemy: nothing will harm you. However, do not rejoice that the spirits submit to you, but rejoice that your names have been written in heaven.

Joy has a lot to do with love and loving one another in the name of Jesus.

In John 15: 9-13 Jesus said;

"As the father has loved me, so have I loved you. Now remain in my love. If you obey my commands, you will remain in my love, just as I have obeyed my father's commands and remain in his love. I have told you this so that my joy maybe in you and that your joy maybe complete. My command is this: Love each other as I have loved you. Greater love has no one than this, that he lay down his life for his friends."

4. Kindness - Kindness is another virtue that is valued by Christians. In Colossians 3: 12-14 the apostles Paul and Timothy writes;

Therefore, as God's chosen people, holy and dearly loved, clothe yourselves with compassion, kindness, humility, gentleness and patience. Bear with each other and forgive whatever grievances you may have against one another. Forgive as the Lord forgave you. And over all these virtues put on love, which binds them all together in perfect unity.

5. Peacefulness - Peace in Christianity is attained through Jesus Christ. In John 14: 25-27 Jesus explains;

"All this I have spoken while still with you. But the Counselor, the Holy Spirit, whom the Father will send in my name, will teach you all things and will remind you of everything I have said to you. Peace I leave with you: my peace I give you. I do not give to you as the world gives. Do not let your hearts be troubled and do not be afraid."

Jesus has mentioned the Holy Spirit several times in the discussions in this book. It is clear that the Holy Spirit plays a very important role as the 'Counselor' that teaches humans what to do. Peace as attained through Jesus Christ is maintained through the effect of the Holy Spirit.

In Romans 12:17-19, the apostle Paul wrote to the Romans;

Do not repay anyone evil for evil. Be careful to do what is right in the eyes of everybody. If it is possible, as far as it depends on you, live at peace with everyone. Do not take revenge, my friends, but leave room for God's wrath, for it is written. "It is mine to avenge: I will repay," says the Lord.

This kind of peace is advise from the apostle to Christians living in Rome to present a good image of Christianity through the teachings of Christ. During those days, Christians were fed to the lions as entertainment in Rome at the famous Colosseum and other places. They were also not allowed to bury their dead together with the Romans. The Christians were forced to bury their dead underground which can still be viewed by tourists to-day at the Catacombs in Rome. Paul's advise was to let the Lord Jesus Christ punish the Romans instead. That advise has stood the test of time and it is indeed visible for all to see. Rome is now the center for the largest of all the Christian Churches, The Roman Catholic Church.

There are about 1.5 billion Christians which belong to the Catholic Church.

Paul's influence is very clear. The choice made by Christ in converting Paul to become his disciple is a sure sign that Jesus Christ had foreseen all these events that would take place 2,000 years later.

Jesus has been referred to as the Prince of Peace simply because his teachings emphasized peace and eternal life. These are probably the most important 'Gifts of God', without peace there is nothing worth living for.

The news bulletins on television and the news papers to-day are full of conflict and war. Mostly in Africa and the Middle East in countries controlled by Islam. In book 2

Muhammad's fight to survive is mentioned. It was his victory in Mecca and surrounding areas, that set the tone for the rest of Islam. They, not only have to convert the faithful, but they must also fight to win in battle. These battles are still raging today.

Jesus never took up arms to fight the chief priests and his supporters or even the occupying Romans. In fact he was totally against violence and judging others, even though the Israelis expected the '*messiah*' to deliver them from their enemies....including the Romans.

In Matthew Chapter 26.....he rebuked Peter for cutting off Malchus's ear when he was arrested at Gethsemane by the high priests, teachers of the law and elders with armed soldiers. Peter had a sword and he drew it and cut off Malchus's ear. He was a servant of the high priest.

He commanded Peter, *"Put your sword back in its place...for all who draw the sword will die by the sword"*.

In Matthew 5:38-39 and 43- Jesus proposed loving your enemy. The old law of *'an eye for an eye, tooth for a tooth, limb for limb'* as written in Exodus 21:22-24 should be changed.

In verses 38-39 Jesus said;

"You have heard that it was said, 'Eye for an eye , and tooth for tooth. But I tell you, Do not resist an evil person. If someone strikes you on the right cheek, turn him the other also."

In verses 43-45, Jesus said;

"You have heard that it was said, 'Love your neighbor and hate your enemy.' But I tell you : Love your enemies and pray for those who persecute you , that you may be the sons of your Father in heaven. He causes his sun to rise on the evil and the good, and sends rain on the righteous and unrighteous."

So the Christians were established on peaceful and a positive constructive environment where you love your enemies as well as your neighbors. It is this faith vs the sword that has won over the non-believers. They do agree that the message of love and peace is something worth believing in. Strongholds like Rome where Christians were killed and persecuted simply fell by faith alone.

When you watch the crowds of Romans and pilgrims flock to the Vatican, in the news broadcasts to-day, to hear the Pope speak or for the election of a new Pope then you get some idea of why faith is stronger than the sword in conquering nations. Jesus was right in proposing that love and peace is the best way for a Christian to behave.

The resulting peace and prosperity as experienced in the Christian Nations of to-day is a Gift of God through the teachings of Jesus Christ.

Not only is God giving his children on earth the gift of peace and prosperity, he has also promised through Jesus Christ, that 'a place' will be prepared for them when they leave this earth.

CHAPTER 6. GOD

In book 1, I tried to explain the concept of God from a Christian and Scientific perspective. In book 2, more information was added to the image of God as viewed by the four major religions of the world Christianity, Islam, Hinduism and Buddhism. In this Chapter, I will try and add more information on what the bible say about God.

In the old testament God is referred to by many names.

1. In the very first verse of Genesis 1:1, God has a second name 'Spirit of God.'

'In the beginning <u>God</u> created the heavens and the earth. Now the earth was formless and empty, darkness was over the surface of the deep, and the <u>Spirit of God</u> was hovering over the waters.

Clearly, God has many forms.

In verse 26, God said; "Let *us make man in our image, in our likeness, and let them rule over the fish of the sea and the birds of the air, over the livestock, over all the earth, and over all the creatures that move on the ground."*

The words used in verse 26 is '*Let us*' which is plural or more than one form of God. This may be referring to God the Father and God the Spirit or Holy Spirit....as mentioned in verse 1. God the Son, Jesus Christ, has not entered the picture yet.

The trinity is only formed by two forms of God.

2. God is also referred to as the 'Lord'.

In Genesis 12:1 it is written,

The Lord had said to Abram, "Leave your country, your people and your father's household and go to the land I will show you.

This was God bidding Abraham who was known as Abram first, to go to the '*promised land*'.

God gave him the name Abraham in Genesis

17:4-5, God said;

"As for me, this is my covenant with you: You will be the father of many nations. No longer will you be called Abram; your name will be Abraham, for I have made you a father of many nations."

The Lord is used throughout the bible interchangeably with God and also made famous in Psalm 23.

The 'Lord' is also used to refer to Jesus Christ, God the Son, in the New Testament.

One of the most important developments in the Old Testament was the handing over of the Laws of Moses to the people of Israel, known as the 10 Commandments. This is one of the important pillars of Christian Laws as it is the basis of laws in most Christian countries in the early days.

The grace of God includes saving the Israelites from bondage or slavery in Egypt and the 10 Commandments was designed by God to help and guide the people in their daily lives.

The 10 commandments given by God to Moses are given in Exodus 2: 2-17. It is written;

1. First Commandment -Verse 3 -*You shall have no other Gods before me.*
2. Second Commandment - Verse 4, 5 - *You shall not make for yourself an idol in the form of anything in heaven above or on the earth beneath or in the waters below.*
3. Third Commandment - Verse 7 - *You shall not misuse the name of the Lord your God, for the Lord will not hold anyone guiltless who misuses his name.*
4. Fourth Commandment - Verse 8 - *Remember the Sabbath Day by keeping it holy.*
5. Fifth Commandment - Verse 12 - *Honor your father and your mother, so you may live long in the land of the Lord your God is giving you.*
6. Sixth Commandment - Verse 13 - *You shall not murder.*
7. Seventh Commandment - Verse 14 - *You shall not commit adultery.*

8. Eighth Commandment - Verse 15 - *You shall not steal.*

9. Ninth Commandment - Verse 16 - *You shall not give false testimony against your neighbor.*

10. Tenth Commandment - Verse 17 -*You shall not covet your neighbor's house. You shall not covet your neighbor's wife, or his manservant, his ox or donkey, or anything that belong to your neighbor.*

The Laws of Moses helped the people live their lives according to this code of ethics. It is an instrument of peace and order and was the origin of laws in Christian countries.

We can safely say that laws are a 'Gift of God', to uphold the rights and dignity of man. Just as the life giving rain and sunshine and the Holy Spirit are gifts from God.

There is a symbolic truth in the salvation of the Israelites from slavery in Egypt, the law and eternal life. They are all actions or goodwill or unearned favor shown by God to uphold the dignity of man. For after his banishment from paradise or the Garden of

Eden, God does show his desire to bring man back to him.

This is one of the reasons why grace was so important to St Paul. He was always wishing grace on the recipients of his letters or epistles at the beginning and the end. We can see why, the grace or eternal favor of God is essential for man's survival on earth and eternity.

We do not wish the wrath of God on anyone. The Roman Empire found out that the wrath of God is permanent. The Christians now rule Rome and the world just as St Paul advised the followers of Christ in Rome. *'Let God punish the Romans....keep yourselves pure and holy in the work of Jesus Christ, the Lord.'*

We can see that natural disasters are terrible and even worse than any man-made disaster. Earthquakes, hurricanes, tornadoes, tsunami, disease epidemics and so on. Are they classified as the 'Wrath of God?'. There is a hint in the First and Second Commandments.... *'Thou shall not have any other Gods....but me'.* Even future generations will be punished for the crimes of the present generation. It is worth noting that the 'Wrath of God' is brought about by the actions of man. Perhaps St Paul should have pointed this out....even though he hinted at it. Rome will fall because *'they are keeping idols and other Gods.'*

Perhaps St Paul knew that the early Christians were not very sophisticated enough to understand more than a few things at one time. He clearly promoted 'grace' or the eternal unearned favor of God above everything else. And rightly so....the Christians of to-day are benefiting from the eternal favor of God. It is there for the whole world to see.

Why are some people fighting all the time? Is it for their rights? Or perhaps they are suffering from the 'Wrath of God'? It is time to stop and smell the flowers, look at the birds and the trees. Nothing is worth living for when you are in a continual state of war. Only God can give you eternal peace through his grace as St Paul pointed out in his letter to the Ephesians 2:8;

'For it is by grace that you have been saved-

through faith, it is not from you but a gift of God.'

When we look at the universe, the stars, planets and the huge amount of space they are floating in, it is hard to comprehend. How vast and complicated it is. There is a force holding everything in place, even though that some space objects move at great speeds, like the comets, but it is all in a pattern and very orderly. It is not chaotic and unplanned like some people propose. An accident of time and space. They are all held together, in an orderly way, by the energy of God.

Only energy is indestructible and conserved. Scientists already discovered this universal truth. Everything is made of energy. Einstein discovered this universal truth, when you convert matter into energy, it is so explosive and with such force that it can be used for good like production of electricity or destruction like atomic bombs.It is a decision made by man. Energy is another 'Gift of God', it is man who decides what to do with it. It is huge and powerful because it is part of God.

It is worth mentioning the relationship between energy and karma or sin. Slowly, we are beginning to unravel God's plans or part of it.

The Hindus believe that when you commit bad deeds, it creates a 'bad impression' which is immediately acted upon by the energy of the universe. Things start to happen because of the negative energy created. The bad karma or 'Wrath of God'. The 'bad impression' is also passed on to future generations....perhaps through the genes to cause problems for them. Hindus believe that physical disease or other manifestations of sin or bad karma are the results.

When you commit good deeds, they produce 'good impressions' which generate good energy in the universe. Good things begin to happen because you have 'awoken' the grace and good will of God. This good karma allows one to escape from the suffering of this world to eternal joy in paradise or heaven or the Garden of Eden.

I believe that the 'energy' which controls the

good and bad karma is part God. It is up to man to create his own future. Either you earn the grace of God and your family and future generations reap the harvests of God's favor or you generate negative or bad karma which will bring your future generations the 'Wrath of God'. So many bad things happen that it will be very obvious even to the untrained.

We know that we can control our destiny. St Paul has pointed this out. We simply ask God for his grace and he will award it. We ask and we will receive. How does it work? Everything that happens in the universe or on earth is recorded. The 'impressions' we produce are recorded in our brains, genes and the 'energy of the universe'.....God....they will either create good fortune (God's grace) or bad luck (Wrath of God) depending on what we did. Whether it was good or bad. This is why Christ warned against 'committing sins' because they create negative impressions in the universe that will devastate and destroy. Even your thinking can create bad 'impressions'. It is important to produce 'good and positive impressions' so that we will receive God's grace and his gifts because they are the things that makes life on earth happy and meaningful.

Does the negative impressions or energy affect the way natural disasters are produced? The bible does point out in many instances including the letters of St Paul that this may be the case.

When man produces so much negative impressions of energy in the form of sin or bad thoughts, it generates negative forces that cause damage or harm. These negative forces cannot be controlled unless you change the force from bad to good by your actions. This is the concept of karma in Hindu religion. It is the oldest of all the religions and contains aspects of all the other religions.

Clearly, the world is controlled by God's Energy. God is Energy. Do you Believe?

What can man do to attract the eternal unearned favor of God?

Generate positive energy that will initiate good and positive things to happen.

CHAPTER 7. DISCUSSIONS

In book 1, the influence of science was discussed. Science is probably the most effective of all man made tools. Since the beginning when man was using stones as tools he has gradually developed better and more effective tools. Science has enabled man to dive and travel under the sea, travel through the air, produce better technology and travel into space and the moon. But how does man come up with these ideas? Ideas that help invent the light bulb for example.

It is said that Thomas Edison tried more than 10,000 different ways of creating the light bulb. They all failed! When he was told he has failed, he replied; 'No I simply found 10,000 ways that did not work'. He was finally successful and invented the first ever light bulb which has changed man's life on earth in unimaginable ways. The earth was enveloped in darkness before and now light in the cities of the world can be seen from space at night. The light bulb is man's invention.

The brothers who invented the aeroplane tried many times before they succeeded.

The Scientist that discovered penicillin had a 'light bulb' moment when he saw the effect it has on bacteria and other micro-organisms. That 'light bulb' moment has changed the world and saved millions of lives. More and more antibiotics were discovered or invented.

But how do these people come up with these brilliant ideas and the knowledge to create something useful out of them? Is it their brains? Which is just a mass of ganglia and tissue and water? They are not intelligent by themselves but are part of man the creator. The intelligent being.

We can use the same analogy in terms of man and God. Man is just a collection of atoms arranged into tissue which, collectively, is known as a person. Where does that collection of atoms get its intelligence? Does it produce it by itself? Does the mass of ganglia, tissue and water in the brain produce all the wonderful and brilliant ideas that has become modern technology? That has produced cities and space travel? Why does that mass of tissue die? At some stage that collection of atoms called man will die and decompose and   become dust.

Man returns to the earth where the bible say he was taken from. So obviously, the soil from which man was made does not have that intelligence.

In book 2, I proposed the concept of the 'Higher Being'. The soul or spirit as it is better known. The driver of the car, so to speak. The entity responsible for man's brilliance. When it leaves the collection of atom that make up man's body, it dies. The atoms return to the earth where they came from.

It is becoming clearer that the 'Higher Being' is the driver of man's success. But how does the Higher Being operate? It seem to be incapable of existing by itself. It has to have a body of a man to function. Without an earth body, it will return to God. It becomes part of God or Energy itself.

This is man's destiny as believed by the

Hindus. That our mission in life is to get back to God. Then why do we need earth bodies in the first place? Why can't we just exist as 'Higher Beings'? All powerful and all knowing like God?

Therein lies the paradox of man.

Why was man created and why does it need God to survive?.

There are a lot of accounts about people who died or were pronounced 'clinically dead' but have come back to life. They say that a powerful light from the sky shone on them and seem to attract them to it like a magnet. Is that the spirit returning to God? There must have been people who died and returned to tell these stories in ancient times as well. This must be the origin of this belief that man will return to God or the Cosmic spirit when he dies. It is not too far from the truth. In fact, this may be the truth. More and more 'clinically dead' people tell of the same experience.

So we do have evidence of man returning to

the 'Cosmic Spirit'.

To answer the question of man's creation, we have to look at the Book of Genesis again at the act of creation itself. It must be that when God created the universe with the stars and the planets they all have a purpose. The planets were created to 'house man and all living things'. The stars were created to feed these living organisms.

Is it not true that God feeds the birds and wild animals? It is true also that God feeds the plants too. God provides the nutrients and water from the earth and sunshine from the stars to help the plants create carbohydrate, proteins, vitamins, trace elements and all the necessary nutrients that animals and man need to survive on earth.

This is the amazing proposition of it all.

Man was created in the image of God, because it is man that generate the energies of God!

How does it work?

The Hindu proposal that our actions produce 'impressions of energy in the universe' is the key to it all. Even man's thoughts produce 'impressions' of energy. These are the driving forces of the universe. Man creates positive energy which generates all the good things on earth. Man can also generate negative energy which create all the bad things on earth. Man is the master of his destiny, but he has yet to control it.

Why? Because man will first have to learn to understand the universe and how to control the energy of the universe. There it is. Man can control what God gives to him. It is through his own actions that the negative or positive energies are created.

One of the laws of motion as proposed by Sir Isaac Newton, one of the most famous of ancient Scientists, is that *'For every action, there is an equal and opposite reaction'*. This law has been found to be true in every case.

But does it apply to karma? Does it apply to man's destiny and the future of the world? To nature and all the creatures of the earth?

I believe so.

It is the actions of man, and even his thoughts, that creates the *'equal and opposite reaction'* from the universe itself. That equal and opposite reaction are the energies that drive everything.

Does the energies created by man drive natural disasters?

The law of energy as discovered by Scientists say;

Energy cannot be created or destroyed, it can only be changed from one form into another.

If this is so and man's action and thoughts 'create positive or negative' energies...then it must be that energy itself is intelligent. Because energy can recognize the negative and positive and reacts accordingly. Thus Energy, in that sense is God, which causes all things to happen on earth and in the heavens.

Man can design his own destiny by creating or changing the energy into positive and negative forces that can either do good or harm. This is the whole point of karma. Your actions will determine your punishment in the next life. You either escape and return to God if you are good, or you get demoted back to earth into more pain and suffering until you learn to be good.

Scientists have yet to study this phenomenon.

There are some who already do in secret. Perhaps Governments who wish to find out how to control the universe through these forces.

We see a lot of these stories and imaginative movies and animated cartoons which depict magicians and sorcerers with powers to change the physical and spiritual world. Maybe such people existed in the past but Government do not want us to know about them or their knowledge because we might become too powerful for Governments to control.

It seems from the theory of it, that man has this power at his disposal but he does not yet know how to control it.

Once man is able to control these forces of good and evil, so to speak, he can control both the physical and spiritual world. Even with his own words, like God himself. He simply speaks and it is created for him. This is what Jesus taught the disciples. They were able to perform miracles in his name with the power of the Holy Spirit.

We have heard of many miracle performers from around the world but they do not seem to understand where their power comes from. Some say it is from God others say something else, more like magic.

This is where Jesus Christ was different from all the other prophets and miracle makers, he was able to control its power. He knew where the power comes from and he was able to transfer that power to others. That is why 3 billion plus Christians believe he was God himself.

In this modern age, man is able to use Science to create just about anything. Man is confident of his powers that Science has given him. He is able to manufacture miracle medicine that can cure many diseases. He is able to manufacture steel, plastic, computers and produce wonderful machines like modern cruise liners and jet planes. Man's computers has created a virtual world called the 'internet' inhabited by digital beings created by himself.

Man is able to find out the deepest secrets of the oceans, the jungles, earth itself. Man is able to do just about anything with his Science. But where does man get his Science?

Science is about a procedure called the 'scientific method'. This method is based on several steps of logic on how to determine whether an observation is true. These are the steps in the Scientific Method.

Step 1. Observation

If I observe that some plants in my crop are 'sick', then I will try to find out why and what causes them to be sick.

Step 2. Hypothesis

Once I have made my observation. I then form a hypothesis or a statement about what is happening to my crop.

Statement;

My crop is affected by a plant disease.

Step 3. Testing the hypothesis.

I will then carry out experiments, further observations and tests to prove or disprove my hypothesis.

Step 3. Proving or disproving my hypothesis.

If, after my experiments, tests and further observations, I discover that a virus disease is affecting my crop then I would have proved my hypothesis to be true. My crop is affected by a virus disease. I will then design control strategies to stop the disease from affecting my crop.

Or I will design and manufacture chemicals to stop the disease if it is a fungus, bacteria or insect.

The same procedure is applied to all manufacturing and production of modern goods. It is only through the scientific method that man can produce 'miracles' by using its logical steps.

Man can produce many miraculous machines, chemicals and medicine using the scientific method.

Universal Truths or Scientific Laws come from experiments using the Scientific method. The result is true all the time and cannot be disputed by anyone.....hence it becomes a universal truth such as the law of energy.

'Energy cannot be created or destroyed, it can only be transformed from one form into another'.

These universal truths or scientific laws make up the knowledge that is indispensable in the world of science. Man is able to manufacture atomic bombs with huge destructive power because of these universal truths or scientific laws. Man can make millions of bombs to the same specification every time.

Man can make cars to the same specification every time. Man can produce huge aeroplanes and giant boats to the same specifications every time. Whatever man makes he already knows the laws that govern the nature of his ingredients, whether they are steel, plastic, chemicals, computers and so on.

That is why man is the miracle maker because he has the knowledge of the physical world given to him by Science.

Similarly, there are laws of the spiritual world. We can deduce these laws of the spiritual world by applying the Scientific method to it. First we make observations, then we test it using logic then we make conclusions about our results. If we find these observations to be true every time, then they should become universal truths about the spiritual world. Why? Because we can see the effects of the spiritual world in the physical world.

Note that universal truths are about characteristics of the physical world that cannot be denied. It is the truth. No one can lie about it or change that truth. Whatever happens in the physical world that truth will always be true.

I believe that in the spiritual world we can also discover truths that cannot be denied. Truths that will remain true all the time. No one can lie about or change it. Whatever happens in the spiritual world those universal truths will always remain true.

These are some universal truths that we can say about the spiritual world;

1. You can change the universal forces affecting you through prayer.

This is why a lot of Christians believe in the power of prayer. When they pray and ask God something, they know when their prayers are answered. It is a miracle that man can perform spiritually. You can speak those desires and they are created for you. Similar to creation, God speaks and it is created. It is a fact of the spiritual world.

There is power in prayers. Where does it come from? Jesus Christ said... *'ask and you will be given'*.

2. God exists.

There are people who deny God exist. They are called atheists.

However, as I have already explained there is no other explanation for the phenomena that we see in the physical world other than the existence of God.

Do you believe that your existence is an accident of nature? That you simply evolved without a plan over billions of years and arrived at the perfect stage you have now? If you do not believe then why is it that you have flesh and blood instead of having part of a tree or other animal attached to you?

For example, part of you will grow branches,

other parts will have fins and you have the mouth of a crocodile? Because they all accidentally arrived there on your body...with no planning whatsoever!

Why is your brain so perfect? Even Scientists cannot explain fully why the brain has so much power! Why didn't you have the brain of a dog or cow? Why do you have a human brain?

Why can the genes store all the information to create a new you which can be stored in many computers! Perhaps thousands of computers will be required to store the information in a single gene!

Why can the body function while it is still alive? Why is it not functioning when it is dead? Why is it dead?

Surely the body cannot function by itself? Otherwise why isn't the dead body walking around and performing tasks of a live person?

It is clear that there is something inside that body that gives it life!

In the movie of creation man was just a pile of dust, then God *"breathed life into it"*. And the dead pile of dust became flesh and blood and a human being.

God had already decided how and what his creation is going to be.

God the Father had declared to God the Spirit. The Trinity.*'Let us make man in our image. Let us make him like us!'*

So man was created like God. That is why man is the miracle maker that he is. That is why man is the creator like he is. Because he was made to be like God. He just have to discover how to use all of God's power by himself! Or he can ask God and God will give it to him.

This is what Jesus was trying to teach the disciples. In the end he send the Holy Spirit to help them. He transferred the power of God to them so they can perform miracles in his name. They can heal the sick and speak in many languages. He has been telling them that they must have faith, they must believe and the rest will be done for them. Like in prayer all they have to do is to speak their desires and it will be as they desired.

That is the power of faith, that can move mountains. That is the power of God that Jesus knew but man cannot understand.

When Jesus fed the four thousand people with a few loaves of bread and fish, everyone who were there were amazed. But they did not believe. The High Priests, Pharisees and their supporters still wanted a sign from God. Even though they have seen all the miracles performed by Jesus, they still did not believe.

Jesus said about their request for a sign from heaven, 'if they cannot believe what they see how can they believe a sign from heaven which they may not see'?.

That is why man cannot perform the powers of God. Even though he can see the miracles of God all around him, he still does not believe.

Like St Peter when he asked Jesus if he can walk on water, and Jesus said yes, but St Peter sank after a few steps because he suddenly does not believe that he is walking on water! Jesus said to him.... 'oh you of little faith'.

When Jesus performed some miracles some of the persecutors of the Christians asked....is he not the kid from Nazareth? Joseph and Mary's son?. They could not believe what he is saying that he is the son of God and was sent by God. Even when he is showing them all the signs from heaven....healing the sick, curing the blind, raising the dead, feeding four thousand people, changing water into wine and many other miracles.....they still won't believe. Thus is the problem of mankind.....they will not become Gods because they do not believe. Only the power of the Holy Spirit will allow them to perform miracles.

Technology in the modern world is moving and developing so fast that very soon the digital products in the virtual world of the internet may come to life as robots. You can send robots attached to an email all over the world. The danger is that it can both be used for good and evil.

Such is the power of man the creator was given to him by Science.

In book 2, I briefly discussed the role of the Holy Spirit in man's ability to perform miracles. Similar to the argument that man cannot exist as a dead body....we can conclude that man.....the dead body.....is made alive and is driven by a 'Higher Being'....namely the Holy Spirit. We all agree that the dead body cannot be a miracle maker. What can a decomposing body achieve? Nothing!

It is only through the power of the Holy Spirit that man can perform all his miracles. It is only through the power of the Holy Spirit that the body is alive and working. The body is made of dirt from the earth and it will die and decompose and become soil again.

Everyone can perform a simple experiment to test this hypothesis. Just put some meat somewhere and observe what happens. After a few months it will be eaten by maggots and insects and only a pile of dirt or soil remains where the piece of meat once lay.

How can a pile of dirt perform miracles? Do you seriously believe that a pile of soil can be a miracle worker? Producing aeroplanes, ships, medicine and all the modern goods we see to-day?

Anyone who believes that must be lacking in the logical department.

God does exist.

God is the energy that drives and holds the universe together.

God is Energy. Do you Believe?

St Paul was the man chosen by Jesus as his instrument to spread the gospel. His epistles or letters are full of revelations from Jesus Christ. His words have so much power in them, we can only conclude that they are the words of the Lord Jesus Christ. Just read his letters to see what I mean.

He was right... *'for it is by grace you have been saved through - faith and this is not from yourselves, it is a gift of God.'*

References.

1. New Testament, Psalms, Proverbs. The Gideons International, 2900 Lebanon Road, Nashville, Tennessee, U.S.A.
2. The Oxford Dictionary, Oxford University Press, London, U.K.
3. The Holy Bible, New International Version. Zondervan Bible Publishers, Grand Rapids, Michigan, U.S.A.
4. Wikipedia, The Free Online Encyclopedia.

www.ingramcontent.com/pod-product-compliance
Lightning Source LLC
Chambersburg PA
CBHW060123050426
42448CB00010B/2005